DIARY OF THE LAST MAN

An established environmentalist, Robert Minhinnick is joint founder of Friends of the Earth Cymru (1984), and the charity Sustainable Wales (1997), for which he is a special advisor.

He edited the international quarterly, *Poetry Wales* (1997–2008), and received a major Creative Wales award in 2008 to write a collection of short stories about refugees, *The Keys of Babylon* (Seren, 2011), shortlisted for Wales Book of the Year.

Other recent publications include the novels, *Sea Holly* (2007 – shortlisted for the Ondaatje Prize) and *Limestone Man* (2015), both from Seren. *Fairground Music: the World of Porthcawl Funfair* (2010) appeared from Gomer.

His poems have twice won the Forward Prize for Best Single Poem and his essays twice won Wales Book of the Year.

A film, *Diary of the Last Man*, made by Park6 Productions, is released in 2017.

ROBERT MINHINNICK

DIARY OF THE LAST MAN

CARCANET

For Margaret

ACKNOWLEDGEMENTS

Versions of some of these poems have appeared in *Modern Poetry in Translation*, *PN Review*, *Poetry Ireland*, *Poetry Wales*, *New Welsh Review*, *Guardian*, *Pivot* (USA), *Cordite* (Australia), *Jubilee Lines: Sixty Poets for Sixty Years* (Faber).

First published in Great Britain in 2017 by
Carcanet Press Limited
Alliance House
Cross Street
Manchester M2 7AQ

www.carcanet.co.uk

A CIP catalogue re

ISBN 978 1 784103

The publisher ack

Supp
AR
EN(

Contents

Diary of the Last Man

    1. *Prophecy*   7

    2. *Snipe*   7

    3. *Slugs*   8

    4. *Oyster Shells*   8

    5. *The Nettle Picker*   8

    6. *Anglers*   9

    7. *Nocturne*   9

    8. *The New World*   9

    9. *How it goes*   10

    10. *Moraine*   10

    11. *The Future*   10

    12. *Plastic*   11

    13. *Home*   11

    14. *Summer*   11

    15. *London Eye*   12

    16. *Nostalgia*   13

    17. *High Life*   13

    18. *At The Grand Pavilion, Brighton*   14

    19. *Cross Country*   15

    20. *And the morning after...*   15

    21. *Isopod*   16

    22. *Pontlotyn*   16

    23. *Sandwort*   17

Suite for Children's Voices and Moog Theremin

    1. *Song of Sleet*   18

    2. *What the Rain Said*   19

    3. *Dark One*   19

Lines for Steve Harris   21

Mouth to Mouth: A Recitation between Two Rivers   25

The Body
1. *With the Body Piercers* — 53
2. *The Penis* — 54
3. *Upstairs at The Beast Within Tattoo Studio* — 54
Morphine — 56
Amiriya Suite
1. *After the Stealth Bomber: Umm Ghada at the Amiriya Bunker* — 58
2. *WMD* — 59
3. *Side Effects* — 60
4. *At a Dictator's Grave* — 61
The Mongoose — 64
The Magician — 65
Leyshon — 67
1. *When the Brandy came Ashore* — 67
2. *Mymryn*
3. *On the Midnight Full* — 70
4. *What Leyshon said he heard at the Prince of Wales* — 71
Aversions — 73
From the Welsh of Karen Owen — 76
'THPW 1921' — 76
Iwan — 76
Salt — 77
From the Turkish of Nese Yasin — 78
Poisoned Apple — 78
Aleysha — 79
From the Arabic of Marwan Makhoul — 81
Jerusalem — 81
From the Turkish of Erozcelick Seyhan (1962–2011) — 82
Coffee Readings 1 — 82
Coffee Readings 2 — 82
Coffee Readings 3 — 83
The Sand Orchestra — 85

DIARY OF THE LAST MAN

1. *Prophecy*

    Perhaps
I am the last man.
Perhaps I deserve to be.
So in this driftwood church
I hum my hymn of sand.
    Yet any god
would be welcome here.
    Any god at all.

2. *Snipe*

Come out of the frozen cress.
Two of them, two lines of barbed wire
across the sky, two voices
with snapped-off vowels, electrical and mad.
Such sneerers, snipe, sulky that I could come
so close to their ruined aristocracy,
rank in its rags. But if I called
I know they would turn back.

3. *Slugs*

I awoke in the dark.
Perhaps I was delirious, but I had dreamed
all the sunflowers were eaten
by enormous mouths. A hundred, I'd say,
gone overnight, and the seeds hardly split.
Yes, I am coming to realise
that the only horrors
are in my head.

4. *Oyster Shells*

Sleet off the sea
blinds the right eye.
Under my boots these faces
of old men at their gruel,
their blue craniums.
Meanwhile the wind is blowing everything backwards
and flaying the duneskins into the sky.

5. *The Nettle Picker*

The next day my fingers throb
pale and purple, the poisoned nerves
at least alive. I took the crowns
with the pollen on them through a mist of webs.
Now, here's a black tonic I stir from a half-remembered spell.

6. *Anglers*

How tedious were the fishermen.
Always the same enticement:
log on, log on, the wonders await.
But I prefer the midnight swell
and the moon that dips its sickle in the surf.

7. *Nocturne*

The clouds flaked with gold leaf,
the sea burning. And I wonder
why I am writing this down,
knowing what I know, dreading what I dread.
Perhaps I should call a truce with myself.

8. *The New World*

This castaway's life? I curse it:
scoffing scurvygrass, burying my scat.
I thought when the smoke cleared
there would be a different world.
But though my driftwood fires
are blue as Sirius
each brings a new apostasy.

9. *How it goes*

Evolution theory suggested we
were once the colour of the sea.
But now we match, it's true,
ash from a disposable barbecue.

10. *Moraine*

A barricade the sea
builds against itself. There's coal in it,
and coral, flints and flinders,
but when I stoop
I stoop for a child's shoe, still laced.

11. *The Future*

Not a soul now,
not a sound.
If it's true I am the only one
then I might move inland,
find a mansion, dine at
the Duke of Westminster's teak table,
lick the paint from his last Lorrain.

12. *Plastic*

White and mauve as a marble Christ.
Here's another god who wanders the world,
its rhizome in the rabbit-hole, its hosanna in the wind.

13. *Home*

But until I know
what the world wants of me
I will stay here, the moon
curved like the conger's tusks,
these waves, dark as marrowbone,
breaking where I know they'll break,
stopping where I say.

14. *Summer*

   I look round:
here's honeysuckle's hooks and sickles.
Meanwhile, the yellowhammer
– little goldsmith of the gorse –
     has arrived.

So, summer's come.
Time to go, I say to myself.
It's what my blood believes.

15. *London Eye*

I come down Regent Street and there's nobody here.
   No,
        no-one here.
                Nobody.
                        The only soul my own.

In the Travellers' Club, room after room of maps
and portraits, empty leather chairs.

This is where the world's wanderers brought their stories,
and behind glass are the explorers' diaries,

blotched by Cherrapunji rain,
pages thick with desert dust.

And such deserts:
Saharan, Sonoran, the thirsty Thar.

Then I picture the caribou-skinned aristocrats,
knocking their pipes out on Greenland's lava.

This is where the idea of Africa
was first conceived.

Though none have seen what I have seen
who is left to read what I must write?

I sit in the travellers' armchair
and sip the travellers' gin.

Yes, today might be the day
when all the great astonishments must cease.

16. *Nostalgia*

The door to 10, Downing Street
is open. In I walk.

The Prime Minister's computer
has a gold screen.
Its password will be his name spelled backwards.

And here they are, the cover-ups, the scandals,
advice on how to smile, how to apologise.
All the meaningless secrets.

And suddenly the tears are running down my face.
Those were the days, I say to myself.
Those were the great days, the last of our lives.

17. *High Life*

I miss the rocks, their ristras
of wrack and the pools where the old
connivings recommence
on every tide,
            the beach at night
with an August moon the colour of coralweed.

Yes, yes. This and that. That and this.
But for now in my suite at the Ritz
it must be the grand cru, always the grand.

18. *At The Grand Pavilion, Brighton*

How calm the dead
        in fancy dress.
Not a look of unease,
        not a sign of distress.

In The Lanes they loll
with mysterious smiles:
        all the young bloods
in their Regency duds
beatified.
        Terrors twinkled away
like froth on a last latte.

But now the party's over they seem relieved,
as if life had been an interruption
in some enormous dream.

Dream easy, I say, to the serene faces,
that become each day, I swear,
more beautiful.

19. *Cross Country*

Yes, this is England, its leas
and leats, its lotteries,
the barley lying flat
behind the Turkish laundromat,
and swifts' black fire
over razorwire.

A military state
through a kissing gate:
such digital riches
but no poets or witches.
Just keep off the grass
says Securitas.

I come over all mardy
in Chorlton-cum-Hardy,
friendless, forlorn
around Sittingbourne,
leery in Leicester
and cheesed off in Chester,
so fazed out in Frome
that I start to walk home.

20. *And the morning after...*

Look at the purple laver:
silk stockings and an evening gown draped over a rock.
Someone had a good time last night.

21. *Isopod*

Gravely we file
through limestone's presbyteries.
Then at 12 o' clock the tide opens its tavern door.

22. *Pontlotyn*

I had relatives here once, a fossil
family, the carboniferous limestone
built into our blood.

We were the cuneiform children
cut into the coal,
scholars who wrote with mattock, maul.

Before that we were
tree orchids, then creatures
that crept through a tropical sea
to be kept as curios
in museum-like front rooms.
No, I think, no, I cannot go back.
The damage runs too deep.

23. *Sandwort*

It was the sea
made them modest.
And how their thirst
thrives.

There's a hill behind us
where corals are kept in cabinets of somnambulistic fire.
All the dead are delivered there,
their algorithms now dust.

Such energy it takes
to make them luminous,
these sandwort flowers
whiter than thistlemilk
or the cuttlefish moon.

It was the sea
made them modest,
as here they wait
lit low on the last of the land.

But here. Always here. A fact
I note as I drag myself out of the waves
towards their atoll fringe.
Alive, I hear a cry go up:
this one's still alive.

SUITE FOR CHILDREN'S VOICES AND MOOG THEREMIN

1. *Song of Sleet*

Sleet I love
in sloomy weather,
the slapdash sky
when we're together.

Yes sleet I love,
indeterminate
urchin, snottynosed
angel on the slate.

Yes sleet I love,
its slide, its slew,
its sleeriness,
dangerous dew.

Yes sleet I love,
silver hermaphrodite,
sly in the wind
her pinch, his bite.

The snow they say
is real weather
but I love sleet
when we're together.

2. *What the Rain Said*

Out of this drout,
one drop, two,
delicious as dew
my waterspout.

Out of the dry
and the desert of my dark dream,
one drop, two, I aim for you,
shaking a shower,
driving a drizzle down your screen.

That's me, scrolling down,
a rough and ready rain today,
right down your neck, I'm pouring down.
But look, child, how I give you,
a silver crown.

3. *Dark One*

Sun-stunned I stare
at sand, at stone.
If I move, the diamonds on my skin
twist like a girl's bracelet.

In my tooth I find fever,
in my coils carry
a cauldron of spells.
Dark one, I deal in delirium.

So what are words to me
or news of the world,
wars and these widows
weeping for warriors?

All history hates
what I must become.
Fire and iron
pursue me to the pit.

Sun-stunned I stare
at sand, at stone.
You are very near now.
Watch where you step.

LINES FOR STEVE HARRIS

1.

Snow.
A red warning,
rare these parts.
The isobars packed black.

Now
a garden full of thrushes
as within our walls the winter redwings wait.

Meanwhile in strata under the ice,
a tea-green marl, with silica wholly crystalline
in double-terminated sharp short prisms...

2.

You daughters and you granddaughters of uranium,
where would we be without...

Hope?
Itself an isotope.

Steve drank the radioactive cola
and then saw revealed that speckling on the scan:
his breast more spotted than the mistlethrush.
No potion-dream this, and the same black messages
along his spine, his hips, then that motley on the ribs.
All across the silver sketching he has now become.

When I held Caryl Ward's hand
    I knew I touched the grave.
    We are ghosts, I tell anyone who might listen.
    We are ghosts.

3.

    Driving Steve to the hospice,
icicles fell from trees on to the windscreen.
Those ash branches were bowed with ice
all the way to Pwll y Mer and its frozen reen.
Dirty bandages, that snow, that morning.

Years ago, when I ferried my father the same way
only one of us returned. But neither guessed the truth.
Now Steve's wife says he already smells of death.
Maybe two weeks, she says, readying herself
to live beyond all this.

    But that scent?
    Is it the sulphur
    in him? The silver?
    In him? The gases
    from the iron star?
    Within him?
    Is it the calcium
    as his bones begin to snow?
    Tell me how the spectra speak.

I know one day
the gold must leak from his pores
and phosphorus leap
out of his mouth in a fiery syllable;
his heart become coral,
cold and curled.

Or is it strontium,
common as cuttle in this world?
Maybe he smells of sand.
Listen, I have breathed
the starlight on Cog-y-brain
  that feeds its fossilbed
  and those shadows
  become bone
  then fossils again.
  And so it goes.
  And so it goes.

4.

Beside this quartz are grains of brown tourmaline
and garnet paler, with vesicles filled with chalcedony.

Steve would sit with coffee
under the mullions of a marine sky,
the fruit machines ringing in the arcade,
maybe one player in that café, sand
on the counter like spilled sugar.
Yet it was somewhere he might work.
And feel glad.
        Because work is prayer.

The fieldfares jostle
frosted. All these slate-shouldered
northerners fled to our salt shore.

You daughters and you granddaughters of uranium,
there is no farewell as you quit your lodgings.
How might the atom
atone?

MOUTH TO MOUTH:
A RECITATION BETWEEN TWO RIVERS

I'm thinking about stars. There is my stargazy mother, almost a girl again, outside in a frost blue as lightning...

Yes, that's... she says... That's... *Alpheratz.* Do you know what Alpheratz means? "The head of the woman in chains." Oh, a rare star, Alpheratz. A double yolker. You must remember when we used to watch 'A for Andromeda' on the BBC? When we were all together and never missed an episode. How beautiful Julie Christie was in her first role...

★

> What I hear
> is the hiss of him.
> His history. Out of a bronze age
> hurtles his brown bones
> but the honey of him is hidden.
>
> Hey, red man.
>   Yes, you red.
> A brazier, I'd say. And brave to a fault,
> my brother of the bracken under the ridge.
>   And here he comes again,
> crossing the sinkholes, those
> chalices of chert and marjoram.
>
> Now watch him wade through the wadis
> between the white willows
> to lie like some dune lion.
>   How he pants in the plantain.
> Where he halts is what yesterday
>   was a green lake,

a lake that appears,
                    disappears,
and moves like a mist out of the moss.

But this is the shapeshifter's country
and today the sun is threatening to burn it back to the bone.
That's what his world is like:
        soon its streams
will become sand's surreptitious fables.
        Yet the red man
        will still loll here,
a quiver of quartzites his fine fur.

He is the latest but not the last –
        a dogfox
        digging in dogroses
until the next time he reveals himself,
        tomorrow in the marram,
        a garnet in the gorse.

                    ★

Pixels of earthshine. A waxing moon in the south-west, polished like pumice. On and off the oyster shell in my palm. On and off that neolithic beacon's mother of pearl, frailer than the tritium of my watch. Impossible to think it ever burned. In darkness now I stroke the shellskin, delicate as an eyelid, delicious as the inner thigh.

                    ★

Yes there it is,
woken in a willow wood.

My flashlight lights the scene,
its beam a spar and the splinters of spars,

skerricks of light that leave me
marvelling at moths and the mosaics of my own skin.

Look, I say to myself
(for who else is here?)

After three thousand years our acquaintance is made.
So I turn to the first empty page in my spellbook.

Oh yes, I know what it is,
a remedy for all that ails us,

the nervous and neurasthenic,
the wounded, the wistful,

for those who have sought
to shuffle out of shadow.

It is growing in a hush
of helleborines. Underwater

it seems. Unreachable
in this nave of night air.

I listen to sap-whine, gnat-tune,
taste nettle pollen pale upon the wood.

But no-one. No-one since
the neolithic has knelt here,

mouth to the madweed, mind unmade,
breathing the fruits of this prehistoric plain.

Then the sleet falls into the north half of my soul.
But in the south half is stillness.

I look up. Against the narcotic sky
are dead trees, old nests.

Deer in the slacks are scittering off,
in the moonlight their scuts gleaming,

and I look at myself from far away
and know there is no next night for this.

It is only the now I can ever have,
my harvest of madweed in the white midnight.

★

That might be Mercury, crewel-sharp. Or ice on barbed wire behind the Blue Dolphin Café. It's a fairground up there, out here, as I walk east over the site, shadows at Trecco become black vacuums behind neon swashes. And the caravans silent. Some are stacked on driftwood pale as ivory, some buried to the axles by the glacier. Yes, everywhere the sand, sucking me in. I curse the world in my corslet of cold.

★

This is where the bodies were found. Where the spelter-coloured Pwll Swil is born and replenished from no known source. Even when dry its gravels are infused with water's perfume. This is how freshwater smells.

★

There's water everywhere,
the paths drowned.

How deep?
          It depends.
I dip my hands and here's one drop
for the departed, its duplicate
for the survivors here.

And the chalkwater chirrs in the dark.
There's moonlight in it, with Jupiter to the south
like a liverish white gout
of solder in the slack.

Something close by is drinking
from this enamel lake.
Something is lapping
the lunar wine.

It might be me,
down on all fours,
my tongue in the sand's navel.

Every path I know
has gone under.
The land devoured.

But didn't Diogenes die
of dodgy octopus?
They delivered him to the dogs
in a bucket of Athenian nightsoil.

So why should I be startled
when the hidden world stirs?

Slack?
      Slake?
            Lake?
Meres and mosses and mirrors and mortuaries.
I wait on the ridge and consider my way.

★

And this is how freshwater tastes. I breathe in its crowbones and its
cressbeds, its phenols and its fennels, its foxblood and its icemelt.
Beneath my feet a sweet aquifer has drawn the boundary with salt.
Yes, daily its dew, duly its dew, daily is its duty done.

★

          Sleet
out of sunlight and the day
losing its identity. Now
rostas of mistlethrushes
are called down to the roosts.

How they burn, these barbarians,
for buckthorn berries in their sunset reefs,
some clerks, these birds, some senators,
but most beserkers, mad
with hunger's amphetamine,
come out of the famished north
to gorge at Cwm y Gaer.

They'll lay up for a spell in the fat harvest,
allow their bellies to swell with buckthorn blood,
the axe not yet, the chipper
not yet, nor men as yet, men in their tabards
bright themselves as buckthorn fruit,
men who will grub up ten years' growth,
chain the copse and drain its orange dregs
from winter vats amongst the vines.

And as the flock floats down
it's almost dark in this ravine
where President Kennedy is driven past,
limousine tyres spurting sand.

And look, the assassin's eye
whitens. There's one amongst us now
crooked as the buckthorn root.

★

I kick over the crests. Crystals in the sand are formal as fossils in their crusted foam. These beaches and dunes are not remote. Yet I have walked their paths conscious that this is unchronicled country. No matter how well I learn the way, that route eventually proves too difficult. Familiar as I think I am with the rocks and slacks, the bracken and the sand, the landscape maintains an unknowableness.

★

But who cared about sand?
Not I. Because they were there.
And then they were not there.

A black chaff around the stacks,
their flight unspooling like videotape
about those limestone stooks.

Choughs, I said. The woman looked alarmed.
Choughs, I shouted, and on she strode,
away from the madman's weather.

They're choughs, I laughed after her,
and this is our chance, to be charged with choughs,
these glossy tumblers, guerrillas of anti-

gravity. One had even touched down
and with its red awl was testing the turf.
What was I but a dog barking in the rain,

watching my sky burn like a tapestry,
a western sky charred by choughs,
each chough a chalice filled with ashes,

each chough a choice of life, of death.
For there come days when we can choose.
And I chose choughs.

*

Lost? No, I am never lost. But frequently mistaken. Commote of
vipers, of tors and twmpaths, the dunes defy predictability even
while their seasons possess an ancient regularity.

And yet, they refuse to be understood. In September, the fellwort will
have appeared. Already in July or August I will have glimpsed the
broad-leaved helleborine, or *caldrist*. If I dig into the sandbanks in
January or May I will discover plastics in their pale ores. Out of that

ground will loom evidence of Napoleonic iron, Tondu brick. At dusk
the shingle will gleam with sandwort like drifts of Styrofoam stars.

★

Turning left
I put the sea behind me.
The sea will be true to itself, I think,
but I am my own betrayal.
Who would recognise me now?

And what are those?
Dead trees perhaps.
No, sticks. Parcels of sticks
as if carried in some parade,
or teazles with that turquoise hair they have,
or bullrushes grown taller
than the ridge that runs between us.

But as I climb I see the buck and his thin hind,
the fawn almost black, sipping
from its own reflection in a pool.

Roe deer, three at least,
roan to rust their summer hides.
But already they are edging away
under the thundersky.

The storm
is any moment now, mauve in the north
and metallic in my mouth, the air
aching with the horsemint I've crushed
coming over this plain, soaking and stung,
stunned to see these deer in the dunes.

The hind's white eyes are scouting round,
her flank a mirror in the murk.
After one hundred years the deer are home,
now stock still again, sensing my stink,
their antlers with the limestone hills between,

two shamen praying to the lightning god,
or so they might well be in this unearthly light,
and the storm that rides the horns of roe deer
darkening the air around a man wet through
in the timothy grass
pretending he's not here.

★

But this is not simply a country meagrely named and recorded. This land resists knowledge. It spurns familiarity. What is rejected is human seduction. These dunes prove unknowable in the ways I wish to experience them.

Slowly, during one of my expeditions, a realisation occurs. Under the willows, deep in mangrove-like woodlands bleached by slackwater, even skidding over the wall-eyed ice and astygmatic glooms of a February freeze, I am not vital to this world. No, I am not important here. I am neither integral nor native.

I might imagine I momentarily contain this world. But this world does not seek to contain me. Even such a relentless trespasser as I have been, determined to celebrate whatever power the landscape possesses, does not belong. Cannot and will never belong.

★

Locked in the lagoon
till the tide turns
are a shadow and a shoal.

I thought they were young bass,
mossgreen, all skin and bone.
But something wasn't right.

Yes, look again.
Locked in the lagoon
till the tide turns
this shadow and this shoal.

How they shot the shallows
craving invisibility
under the secret shelves.

Lug dug from their lairs,
swaths of wrack the tide ripped from the rock,
a Christmas tree, a caravan, a plastic machine gun.
All tributes the storm has left
to some greater god.

Shad, surely,
sharp, shaley
under the limestone overhang.
Yes shad. Shuddering
at my shape. They should be extinct:
or top of the Red List.

But these persist;
coldwater pearls
or film stars' handprints
at Grauman's Chinese theatre
filled with morning rain.

So, look again.
Locked in the lagoon
till the tide turns
this shadow, this shoal.
When I'm gone they will come out of the shade:
shrunken. Shrewd.

★

No matter how often I come here, I am destined to remain not only a stranger, but something more profound: a foreigner. As foreign as everyone else who has ventured here: the lovers, the solitaries, the naturalists, the soldiers, the wimberry pickers: everyone as far back as the first people recorded, a clan who camped around a freshwater spring that became 'Ffynnon Pwll'.

★

Cold?
As if from snowmelt:
but green, soon serpentine,
the river out of the reeds.

And I?
Unsure
where the shore starts, a crazed
country this under a sintered sky,
coke in its pyres and pyramids.

Around here they'd put
the *mola mola* in some glass case.
As if it was freakish,
                    but us not:
as if it was fearful:
                    but not us.

No. Never us.
As if there was nothing wrong with how we live,
who have inherited every ounce and inch,
all the suzerainties of the sand.

There is always the sin of strangeness here.
And how soon the sunfish
flesh rolls in on a woebegone tide.
The unrecognisable refugee.

                    ★

But those familes feasted on plovers' eggs and sucked the hauberks
of great green crickets. On their fires they roasted black adderskins
patterned with gorse petals. Yes, those people moved as silently as
the sand itself, the sand that pittered like a rainstick, grew dense
as ant clouds. They buried their dead in a ravine, the adults tiny
as children. And before them passed other generations, unnamed,
unknowable yet...

                    ★

As I was coming up the slope
he stood on the crocket of the dune.
Above us a release of steam
was blowing east. And east meant cold.

A strange encounter
in threatening weather.
Surely he had thought
no-one but he would be out today.

In that sand
he waddled like a raven,
grunted too, as a raven grunts,
when it's on the ground.

There he stood, small head,
big pelvis. A boxy
man built like a cement mixer, silly
willy blue as a mussel shell.

He was coming down as I was going up.
But the works loomed above us both,
ugly as Chernobyl, empty as Ys,
the quench towers, the cooling towers
over the sinter-coloured sea.

And I think now, maybe he was fighting back
in the only way he could,
a dog soldier from the painted tribe,
still refusing to give in.

★

Maybe I might call the first people here my ancestors. Perhaps I require such a thought as solace for myself. But, like me, those ancestors did not belong. Even when they died and the sand packed their brainpans and whistled through their bones, they did not belong. Because belonging is a pipedream. The human condition is one of singularity. The human fate is loneliness.

1.

In the end they hung the magician
in a net from the workhouse ceiling,

his sores like stars, his cries
that familiar language:

cats, buzzards,
the throat's mewling

we all have to learn.
Word perfect.

2.

Old man in your hammock
rock yourself under the limestone sky

while the dark creeps in and creeps away again.
Not ready? Not fit?

Your time is
over. Holy writ.

3.

What made this world, father?
Who trawled you up from the ocean floor –

a coelacanth
out of the purity of prehistory?

From the corals you came,
the commotes of starfish.

So where's your spell for this, then father?
Where's that mysterious book you have been writing.

What's on
the last page, old man,

as you turn
with the mothers of pearl,

as you burn
like all the driftwood kings?

4.

Yes, here's a predicament.
Get yourself out of this one, father.

In your net,
aswing from the raw clevis,

do you dream of one last campaign?
A penthouse in the Brazilian rain?

Too late, old man. Seek no relief.
But the lark will sing in its glory and its grief.

Now, when I place my ear against your mouth,
tell me the questions I'm supposed to ask.

＊

The *unbelonging* I sense in this landscape between two rivers has become an insistence. Yet, I greet it with something that feels like relief. How many years has it taken me to welcome this region's rejection. To embrace the fact that I cannot find myself here? And yet...

＊

Forty years
since I brought that letter home
and who was it from?

Pressed on me in the post office,
by someone saying *this is for you*
was a cream envelope, with, handwritten, our address.

Dannie Abse?
We both already knew that name.
I slit it with my fingernail, craned to see,

and yes, I thought,
I can. I hope
I can.

Now forty Septembers later
I'm on the hot quilt of the dunes,
not far from where you sit

in the Grade Two-listed mansion on the hill,
higher even than the Star Chaser,
our newest fairground ride.

And no, I won't say this place can feel remote
because you would only think
it dangerous.

But I pass quietly, I promise,
quiet on the slopes
and quiet through the birch

struggling out of scree,
quiet where they found those dead people.
Only one thing is quieter now

and we both understand what that must be.
I even passed over the pheasant feather
when once I might have worn it in my coat.

I'm here to look for blinks
that swarmed last year
over the swale at Pwll Swil.

Too late, it seems, they're gone another year.
Fainter, those flowers,
than the stars we'd glimpse under Orion,

low on the southern horizon,
smoky as the seeds I stirred today out of the grass.
How the world ripens

in this dry month,
such a gorgeous toxic blush
with all the mauves of Michaelmas.

But those blinks
were almost impossible to see.
You're in a room I know so well,

whispering through the galleries
of ghosts. Last hours, I think
of this desert month, oh,

and just to say,
that Dannie Abse
died. Was it yesterday?

The night before?
I said something on the radio.
Ninety-one, we calculate,

and his hair like thistledown or rosebay
in its rags. Fireweed its other name
for the tenacity it can show.

But I'll tell you more of that
when I call in after this slouch through the sand,
with other news tomorrow.

★

Now, what comforts, is the awareness that I can never be at home here. Thus, at last, I understand where I am. Finally, the sand makes sense. Only when I accept alienation, my *strangerness*, this *strangerdom*, can I become free.

They brought him up through the runnels and delta gravel,
three men out of their skiff
with last light behind them in the south,

three men with the king on their shoulders,
the scabrous daddy with his wounds, his ulcers,
but the skin of his belly still candle-smooth,

a conger out of the wreck on the reef,
lugged from his lair under a ship's boiler,
visible from shore, that copper kettle,

red and barnacled, viced in the crevice
where the conger lived, the eeltrunk upon
Cornelius's shoulder, under Tudwg's arm,

the head hanging over Dewi's oilskin,
the head they will boil to expose the jaw,
dislocate and wedge wide that jaw,

till the mythological tusks
are bared on Traeth yr Afon
through a night of fire and boasting –

which are the first seedstock of poetry –
the driftwood pyre a ruined hull,
their beerbottles hissing in a gemstone bed.

★

I think of how history has happened here. The sandhills have boasted few historians, fewer bards. To the west was catastrophic inundation. And yet there is evidence of inhabitants who flourished thousands of years ago. Their footprints are visible in peat at the lowest of tides.

★

1.

Look at these.

Thaw sweat.
Smoke on the swale.
Swarf off a swollen sea.

2.

No.
These. World famous
footprints at low water. Nine
thousand years old, they say, but who's
counting. Not me.
Yet maybe I am.

3.

A small man. Or woman. Outcast
or outlaw, hunter, flintknapper, cook.
All of these.

Yes, a woman, pregnant once again,
and coming home through the red mud.

4.

Or maybe she was dancing.
        Yes, a woman, I guess,
who loved to dance
and paint her eyes with kohl and ochre
and squat to squint at herself
in some rock pool and ask
"what are you?"

5.

At night before she slept
she would breathe her harsh
hashish and tell her story behind the flames
about the brine-bright animals
she had scratched into the sand,
her wolf,
       her bear,
             her rhinoceros.

Yes, an armoured rhino
like the torrent poured golden
and smoking from the blast furnace ladle,
a rhino on the glacier coming out of the sun,

a rhino she will picture
with her goatwillowstick
on the last morning she will wake.

To the east was a slower scouring. But in both dunelands, divided as they are by the town, there is dearth of recollection. It is as if sand has concealed more than our limestone ridges and medieval field systems, reaching higher than the coral alphabets that crown the coigns of Cog y Brain. Where the future is written....

★

This woman I pass, let me
praise her proletarian
skin, her smell of raspberries.

But the air darkens.
It is an owl I have disturbed in daylight,
an owl moving away

unreachable as my own breath.
And still the steelworks floats in fog,
a burning city overhead.

The dune is a dangerous journey down,
but here at last are the huts, the refugee
village hidden where the dram road ends,

where there are movers in the mist,
people who persist
in speaking their own languages

and dreaming their own identities
under the venting flame.
All such wretched

radiance is what the owl sees,
that little bishop
out of sand's raw republic.

*

Yes, the simooms have poisoned the plover pools, torn plastic and
slate. But while remembering the past I visualise the storms of the
future. And understand that one of the powers of sand is that it can
obliterate memory itself.

Pausing, I find reciting my lines resuscitates my soul. But who is this
figure in broken boots and carboot coat, talking to himself? Maybe
I should wonder why he draws such comfort from the sand's dream
of extinction.

*

Careful now, I could break my neck. So when I step I am meticulous
as a Babylonian astronomer pricking the clay, naming the cuneiform
constellations, the logarithms of locusts. That old man is a reed that
writes and never rests, his stylus hung around his neck. And I realise
that man is myself, a clerk of the gods who groans in the granaries
of his words.

*

Birch sap's still in spate through spouts and sprues
but spring's the furthest
horizon away.

Here are August ants, their swarm
like swarf over my boots.

I've come across this country
– burnt, besieged –
yet believe I belong here

amongst nits, nettles,
the glumcock, the pink of god,
the pits where gravelers stood their ponies
and warreners skinned coneys
in sand-bitter burgages.

And sweltering, stop.
To listen while a silence creeps
into my bones.

Behind my eyes
that silence sows its unseen suns,
might halt the secret shuttle of the blood.

Ahead
      plastic builds atolls
and archipelagos
      but I sit beside my campfire
      under the fairground stars.

★

His eyesight is dimmer now and he waits with the sun at his shoulder, building the lore. The law. All he knows is that he must pass the lesson on until one evening he is laid upon the current, fireflies over the river. The words are changing yet the last thing he understands is that words can never change. There are dicemen and beggars at Ishtar now, the watchmen and warriors he remembers have vanished under the sands. But the vermilion varnish will linger forever upon his fingernails.

★

In the ward she was hung from wires
and the wires were hung upon her.
Black roses. White thorns.

Then dawn and a hypertensive
winter in her veins.
What's for us who are left?
Debris of daybreak
and the sea full of sharps.

How can this be?
I search but she is already gone.
The cave she lived in?
The sea rinses it twice daily with its furious housekeeping.

★

Before me the cavern is worn smooth
by high tide. But at low water
I ask: where is her flannel?
Does it still bathe the flame of her face?
Are her books upon their limestone sill?

All that remains is a stopped watch, white as an ammonite.
If I close my eyes I might glimpse the road she took,
easing herself out of the hospital bed,
safe at last in the surf.

There's a shape. Dark against the night this shape above my head.
And I think, it is my mother who leans over me, stroking my brow,
who cups my forehead in her palm.

There are so many wrecks on this headland. And people from those wrecks: *The Amazon* whose captain was bound to the mast under the double top gallants, his body not found for nine days; the woman washed ashore still clasping her child; another whose fingers were sliced off for the rings she had slipped on that morning. While here is the deckboy and the donkeyman greaser, the Samtampa iron after all these years, old as the stone itself.

When I put my ear to the rock I hear them all, Captain Garrick calling orders that became his prayers, the women bred on salt and scurvygrass who tied brands to cattle horns.

I've seen bluestones sailing past this desert, then ships carrying silk and apricots, their brandy in imperial measures, *one hundred and ten gallons, sir, in every barrel.* Men died here of such surfeit. One cask could suckle an army and not even the riot act stop those people drinking...

Behind the beach a hurricane tide has sliced the dune in half.
Done as if on a lathe. Now naked in the sand marram roots metres long their swatches ripped, then beams from some past effort at shoring the shore, indecipherable footings punctured with stripper bolts.

Even the moraine has migrated further down the coast, enormous pebbles shrugged aside. Nothing fast here. Because in the dune nothing stays a secret long.

What remains is quartz in the cave, yellow as turmeric. But who dares step in between engulfments? The cavern walls are so slippery only a fool would venture into that hollow world. Entering is child's play. But to emerge...?

You're warm, my mother says.
Warm as a brandy glass.
Maybe you have the fever, she adds.
So many have that fever now.
Everyone is warmer today.
It's a world of delirious children.

★

Moon sharp as a willow leaf. Frost fearful, black and feral. Yet I am at Babylon once again, a breeze rustling in the palm branches, the Milky Way a pale Euphrates. And in the distance, laundrywomen are singing in the shallows, their suds winking between the riverstones...

Note: *The rivers are the Ogmore and Cynffig in south Wales. I encountered the fox in the first poem very close to the 'ancient monument' at Ffynnon Pwll. I was astonished at the animal's colour. It glowed bright as a winter marigold. No urban mange there but robust health. It lay sunning itself on a slope of Cog y Brain, the most substantial summit of the dunes.*

THE BODY

1. *With the Body Piercers*

There was nowhere else to sit
so I sat in the darkness with them

and listened to every word of it –
their 7 pm after work conversation.

And it seemed no different
from all the other conversations

taking place at 7 pm in the world:
that the job was thankless;

that the public was a conspiracy of fools;
that they were paid much, much too little.

And as my eyes grew used to the darkness
I understood to whom I was listening:

they were the ringed and the chained;
they were the studded and the spiked.

There were curtain hooks in their tongues;
there were amethysts in their mouths;

there were daggers through their breasts;
there were golden serpents that disappeared into their navels;

there were ingots in their ears;
there was astronomy in their noses;

there were padlocks on their eyes;
there were needles through their nipples

threaded to silver pulleys
that carried heavier and heavier silver hippopotamuses;

there were wedding rings through their foreskins;
there were swastikas in their labia.

When they had all gone
I looked at myself in the mirror:

I saw a man by himself in an empty room
tapping a pen against his teeth.

2. *The Penis*

Eye to the earth
I'm in disgrace
but point me at the stars
you'll count a constellation in my jaws.

3. *Upstairs at The Beast Within Tattoo Studio*

Ah, lover,
bend slowly over,
look for religion down on your hands and knees

and feel a mazarine blue butterfly
extinct in this country for one hundred years
alight on your right buttock.

Sister,
over your shoulder
a dolphin will bare its knuckleduster teeth.

And sir,
your torso
should be more so.
Across those plated pectorals
I'll commence my Book of Kells.

Who dares
upstairs
to the scriptorium
where Leonardo consults the hexagrams, Celtic DNA?

This needleworker
never slurs a word.
Feel his hypodermic
sip like a hummingbird.

Soon,
around town,
your children will sport his biographia.
Out of the storybooks will step your young
like little blue dragons following their dam.

MORPHINE

for Howard Bailey

All that's in my head is in my head.
Try to notice Neptune, the poet said,

but there's a mist outside, white on a white sky,
warm air across cold sea, turning the world invisible.

Morphine is a sister, is a saint.
In our blood and history they'll trace the taint,

while all I see is the needle plunge,
or the golden-green, green-golden

draught in the eye-dropper
turning the world invisible.

Now a waitress brings the tables in.
I ask her for a napkin

and she comes across to the only customer
talking to himself and writing signs

like the moon and stars, the comet's lines,
as if they could light up the gloom,

or the churning fret that hides the Seagull Room
and turns the world invisible.

I'm just the latest mad bastard to make her day.
But don't worry, I'm not going to stay.

Yet all this dark matter is in my head,
and Howard, now you are forever dead,

and morphine's still a sister and a saint
and an executioner. Too early for a cool carafe?
Let this eye-white fog then be your epitaph.

1. *After the Stealth Bomber: Umm Ghada at the Amiriya Bunker*

It is years later now
but time can also run backwards.
Still she squats in candlelight,
Umm Ghada in the caravan,
or in 125 degrees Fahrenheit,
a cockroach ticking on her divan.

At night
they come out of the bunker,
the children, the old people,
but all a fog of flesh.
One body with four hundred souls
is exposed in a photographic flash.
They pick the wedding rings and wisdom teeth
from crematorium ash.

Who was it dreamed a stealth bomber?
Stealth steals.
Think of a smart bomb.
Not so smart.
Where the missiles entered Amiriya
daylight was star-shaped in the sarcophagus,
the concrete blasted back,
all the bodies foaming like phosphorus
in a bunker in Iraq.

The old women
took off their shoes
to welcome the fire that jumped into their mouths.
How quickly their children
found themselves unborn.

Yes, stealth steals.
But still Umm Ghada
guards. Umm Ghada
who goads God
with her grief
and the ghosts she carries,
Umm Ghada my guide
in the charnel house corridors.

What is she but a woman
in desert black.
Yet no desert was ever so black
as the sackcloth that Umm Ghada owns.
Not the Syrian desert's
Bedouin black, its cairns
of cold stones.

Note: *The Amiriya bunker in Baghdad was destroyed by the USAAF on
February 13, 1991. Over 400 civilians were killed. Umm Ghada, who lost
many members of her family in the destruction, became a guide at Amiriya,
living on the site.*

2. *WMD*

We went to the convent and dug in the tomb.
There were lilyroots concealed in that sepulchure.

We halted the shepherd and looked in the mouths
of his goats. Their throats were gunbarrels.

In Babylon the computer viruses
were laughing at us all the way down Procession Street.

Within the crater of Babel
not a word was left upon a word.

In the refrigerator in the Ministry of Information.
grew a blue bacillus.

The rats in the Tigris were stoned on nerve gas
and in the market by the basilica

a farmer had written nuclear formulae
on the skin of a watermelon.

In the forbidden district
under a picture of Saddam

I peered into the hands of a beggar.
The grey dinari were pages of a book she was burning.

And believe me, I'm still looking. I am still looking.
In my mind I know exactly where they are.

3. *Side Effects*

Sunlight in the public bar
falls white, armorial upon him,

this Barryboy, 5'8"
in phoney CK sweatshirt,

scalp shaved to a badgerstripe,
this Blindfire chucker at Saddam.

First one in, he sits alone,
and yet there attends

anthrax at his left shoulder
whilst plague is patient upon the right:

this fatman with an empty glass
under military escort.

4. *At a Dictator's Grave*

Yes, this is what happens
when the old men make us wait.

And it crossed my mind in the cemetery
about the best way to behave:

how should I conduct myself
beside a dictator's grave?

Someone has left dandelions
in a jamjar. One o clock, two...

Yes, it's later than we think, now lover,
much later than we think.

Because this is what happens
when the old men make us wait.

Yes this is what happens
when the old men make us wait.

And it crossed my mind in the cemetery
about the best way to behave:

how should I conduct myself
beside a dictator's grave?

Why not ragwort, lover? Ivy?
Or the corpse-colour of henbane?

But crowding round, the children laugh
as children always must,

I suppose they'll still be laughing, love,
when you and I are dust.

Yes it crossed my mind in the cemetery
about the best way to behave,

but why did I not use bare hands
to dig the dictator's grave?

Because this is what happens
when the old men make us wait.

Yes this is what happens
when the old men make us wait.

I dreamed I saw our leader, lover,
as he was driven from the scene,

mottled like marble in the back
of a German limousine.

Yet all our lives we've had to drink
green water from the grave.

Yes it's later than we think, now lover,
much later than we think.

THE MONGOOSE

Last night no moon
but one shoulder of Orion.
Now dawn has drawn me down
to the modem and its madnesses,
the water cooler's air kisses.
Above, a roof of strangers in thick sleep,
computers snapped shut like steel snares,
the hookah and its bulb on the dining board,
tobacco cut with lemon and mint.

Outside, the ocean
is the corner of a page, turned up,
an inky fold of the Arab sea.
And once again she is impatient for me,
crouching for coffee grounds and crusts.
There my slattern waits, sleek as a snake,
a thief from the thicket slid into the sun,
but queen enough for a world no god would make.
Zichon Yaakouv

I hang mugwort from my mirror, he says.
To keep evil away? I suggest.
No, he smiles. Because its gold dust on the bevel pleases me.

Also, I dry mugwort in the kitchen.
To stop the quaking? I ask. The terrible tremens?
The hosts of hysteria who beset us all these days?

He seems surprised. For its aroma, he says.
I prefer it to wormwood and the silver salvias.
Though savoury I suppose must run it close.

Upstairs, he says, I pile up pillows stuffed with mugwort buds.
Ah, I reply. A cushion for good conscience?
To nix our nightmares, our dreams of chase,
those feverish frustrations?

No, sir. I sleep soundly. Drowsing in its down till dawn.
And here, look. It grows beside the door.
So that lust does not enter? I whisper.
That dark angel daubed with unholy dew?

Not at all, he smiles. I stand most evenings in the porch
and breathe its oil, the moon in the south
and moonlight the colour of mugwort on the surf.

But look, I say. Your garden's full of it.
Surely for potions and infusions?
To keep fleas away, and nits and gnats,
and the phantoms that would haul us all to hell?

My lawn's a law unto itself, he laughs.
Though sometimes, yes, I will add it to my beer
and sit and sip and sympathise
with all who have called these four walls home.

They will bury me with a branch of mugwort
pressed into both cold hands.
Then to paradise you will go, I cry.
That I might be sweeter, he smiles, on the day my bones burn,
and my friends stand and wave farewell with a simple fern.

1. *When the Brandy came Ashore*

The dead Napoleon, he said,
or maybe it was Nelson,
was preserved from the Mediterranean sun
in a brandy barrel. And yes,
I've heard sailors in their cups
talk of tapping the admiral.

Look, he said, if it was good enough
for old Horatio, or those Spanish monks
and Russian vintners,
why not the likes of us?

So when the brandy washed ashore,
we watched him broach the cask,
push in the bung, and lie down beneath it,
an iron-coloured liquor draining into his mouth:

A hot iron,
        a red hot iron
a red hot iron that brands the soul.

And he stayed there. Thirsty, we thought.
Gulping like a baby at the tit.

After five minutes we looked at one another,
pulled him out from under
and stood him on his feet.

He started to walk home, then turned round.
He said he had read Moby Dick,
seen the black albatross, the white porpoise,
sailed as Mate on the Speedwell with Mr Coleridge,
the poet from over in Porlock,
sailed all the way to Malta.
And for twelve nights, he said, Mr Coleridge
had been provided, by surgeon and captain,
with a brass enema.

A hot iron,
a red hot iron
a red hot iron that brands the soul

Then Leyshon raised his hand,
saluted, and fell down.
Dead. Stone
Dead.

But hot. Redhot his forrid.
I stroked it. Hotter than a brandyglass, I'd say.
A fool in his fever lost forever
in Valetta's honey-coloured stews.

What they put on his gravestone I don't know.
Hero, maybe. Explorer.
Perhaps buccaneer who drowned hisself in brandywine.
Yes, here. On this sand.
I reckon just about where I'm standing now.

2. *Mymryn*

Leyshon talked that night,
the night before they hung Mymryn, the horse mutilator.
Thirteen years old. A dung-coloured child.

No-one spoke for him. But Leyshon translated,
so it was a fair trial. Leyshon claimed
too many had swung on the gibbet at the Prince,

meeting their god
in the wrong language.
But when Leyshon commanded the hearth

no-one had the heart to stop him.
The usual group of us,
but was I the only one listening?

He talked about a beach where he once walked,
covered, he said, in leaves of pink cuttle.
Outside Adelaide, he said, there were iron boulders

in the desert, brought on ox carts to the city.
And when he was lost there were natives
who picked him sweet little peaches.
Quondongs he called them.
Either the peaches or the people.
Saved his life.

Mymryn was shackled and locked in the stable,
two soldiers in rags at the door.
One of the troopers had been at Waterloo,

an old timer, not a tooth in his head, musket broken.
And Leyshon told his tales. Claimed to have once sighted
the ice of the southern continent,

the colour of a sbrocsyn's egg.
It was Leyshon who took beer to the guards,
with a plate of cheese and damsons.

Then, about dawn, we stirred ourselves.
There was a small crowd, and
when they brought the boy out I stood next to Leyshon

and dug him in the ribs.
Listen, I said. It's white, not pink.
So it is, he smiled,

as the boy's neck snapped
like cuttlebone.
So it is.

3. *On the Midnight Full*

I wish old Leyshon could have seen this.
The Megablitz on fire against the sky
and children with their hands full of benzedrine
   rainbows,
and skeletons scratched in the sands,

and the pneumatic music that lifts aloft
all the iron manhole covers,
and all the old men dressed up as Elvis
singing love me tender love me true,
and all the young men standing at the Buccaneer entrance
making their plans for the night, their plans for the night.

Yes I wish old Leyshon could have seen
all that's been happening in his world.
But there's one last fisherman out on the midnight full,
his net dragging home the silver pouting,
back to the town he left two hours ago.
Won't someone tell him that those two hours
might be two hundred years. Yes, two hundred years.
And that everything is changed now. And changed utterly.

4. *What Leyshon said he heard at the Prince of Wales*

                    Voices, he whispered,
Coming out of the walls.
As if language was trapped in the stonework.

So he'd sit all night
by the fire in the old *Prins*
listening to the conversations of ghosts.

Could it be, he once asked,
that words were the mortar
that held all this together?

That there were words floating around us,
and we were like sparrows,
bathing in their dust?

Yes, that was Leyshon. A dreamer.
He used to tell me about a Maltese woman
who worked at the theatre in Old Mint Street,

selling olives from her pinafore.
When he stroked her neck
her hair was coarse as candlewick.

She used prickly pear juice to make it shine.
One evening, he said, there was
gold leaf on her shoulders

that had fallen from the *paradiso*,
gold dust on her eyelashes
and gold lay in a film upon his wine.

Yet the sea had taken him away from us.
He learned its different worlds.
Leyshon the liar they called him,

but I say he should have
never come back to this place
between the rivermouths, disturbing the peace,

conversing with spirits as if they were old friends.
I've listened myself, ear next the wall.
It's a crypt in there, I told him. Not Drury Lane.

AVERSIONS

Versions of the Welsh, Arabic and Turkish

from the Arabic of Fatima Naoot.

Boy

He strikes a match
and is brave once more.
Now, who cares about the bombings and the war?
As long as fire shields shadows
he will not fear Pharaohs.

Girl

The revolution
was a long time ago.
It only makes her yawn.
But when she skips she feels the whole green earth
and is glad that she is born.

Decision

When all else fails
a woman still has her fingernails.

The Sand Station

The world will be a poorer place tomorrow.
Before he has the chance to open his newspaper
in his favourite seaside café,
immediately after the first sip of coffee,
the Devil will die.

And life will be less
without him. From now on
who will care if I claim
to be better than my jealous friends?
Who will I have to blame
for the toothache that swells my jaw?
The story that Satan lived in the dirt of our fingernails?
It was an old wives' tale.

But think of Christina.
She died too, and nobody came.
Christina died lighting the Christmas tree
in a room where a poem is hung on an ebony frame.
How Cavafy had adored her young girl's gaze.

Because women
die. Cavafy's lovers
died. Into the dark
without protest they go,
those brides in black.

So we sit in the Elite café
considering the coffins that will contain us all,
even the fishermen who haul
whole shoals to the harbour steps
and have dulled themselves to death.

Now it's our duty to devise
a funeral for the deceased Devil.
Think of the mourners we'll meet:
my father, who courted my mother for two lovesick years;
my mother who found a physician
to place a wafer of words in my son's mouth.
Even the shoemaker who scattered hobnails in the street.
And I'll be there too, of course,
silent, serious, receiving the condolences
a widow expects.

from the Welsh of Karen Owen

'THPW 1921'

One night, in a barn in Wales,
a poet who sang of Rio
showed how by carving his initials in a rafter
he might evade that void of the hereafter.

Iwan

My wineglass is empty without Iwan.
Seldom and secret
the meetings we made,
soon over, my sole solace.
He was a ghost gone before he'd arrived,
unready for rendezvous
and filling our future with his farewell.

My wineglass is empty without Iwan.
Jaunty, that jut of his hat,
and, despite his griefs,
his muses were as many
as there were motes in the sun.
Yet it was people who lit his language,
raw as the rhythm of his bass guitar.

My wineglass is empty without Iwan.
Now the syllable
of silence perfects the poem.
But what is the soul's silhouette?
Everything now is echoes and exits
except for his shadow, turning away.
My wineglass is empty without Iwan.

Salt

Inexhaustible, the salt
of tears and tides;
it's a slow lesson learning
what time decides.

★

from the Turkish of Nese Yasin

Poisoned Apple

Maybe I existed once upon
a time. Because once upon a time
I was invincible. Or invisible.

The pearls on my pillow
were stony eyes.
                How they stared
into my stunned soul.

Yes I was the spirit
spat from my mother's mouth.
But birds were my breath
and their forest no foe.

At midnight a madnote.
                   How the willows
wailed in the whirlwind
as this waif suckled wolfmilk.

But isn't God always
the creepy stepfather – his eyes a hurt
and hot within the dark?

Yes I have been sleeping the poisoned apple sleep,
my mother missing, my lover lost.
I am a body embalmed in ice.

When I move my mouth
some stranger steals my words.
My own voice is the source of vice.

Inside my maze a sad
museum, every exhibit
a woman's wounds

while out in the orchard
the woodcutters
sit muttering of murder.

Aleysha

There was a time we had a daughter
who was always bouncing on our bed.
She was called Aleysha. Or something like that.

All that life seems a fairystory my mother taught me.
Words were weapons we seldom used,
and the house was a haze of haschich,

and our horizon the bedsheet.
Sometimes, in my crimson dress
I would visit your room

but you were engaged in some holy war
and I felt futile in your fury.
Then your words were woundbringers, bald

as blades, translated by your harlots
and your houris and your whores.
Yet our daughter was adored.

She lifted a ladybird, red and black,
to hold as high as her heart.
That was Aleysha, delightful

as dew, speaking her ladybird language.
I thought it forever, that storybook.
But you were the torturer who taught me

all about rage and wretchedness,
until Aleysha would come and join our hands,
or run after you with naked feet, imploring eyes.

That pleading little peacemaker.
Aleysha? Yes, I think that's how she was called.
A name I might find in a storybook.

★

from the Arabic of Marwan Makhoul

Jerusalem

My journeys to Jerusalem
were not governed by God.
Not for me the city labyrinths
swarming with ghosts
and memories of murder.
Instead, my Jerusalem knew
the justice of evening jasmine,
wine raised for the taste of life itself.

And yes, I once found that taste there
with a girl; forbidden to me,
foreign. How she would fascinate.

Until weekends when the crowds arrived,
scanning scriptures in the alleyways
and the cracks between stones.
All day those scholars thrashed the dust
for proof of the holy signature
that I might imagine in a kiss.
But with my girl gone, Jerusalem
was a jail. My devotion
died on the streets of the devout.

from the Turkish of Erozcelick Seyhan (1962–2011)

Coffee Readings 1

People stand on one another's shoulders
and soon are a tower stretching into the sky.

At the summit, a single hand
silver as a flying fish.

But none of us is last. All of us are first,
as we rise like incense through the sky,
people who become a plume of smoke.

Or, more like a rainbow, or the roads
of a rainbow, its open roads to emptiness.

Surely this smoke now makes a saint,
a smoke-saint who is a smoke-man or smoke-woman too,
all of us writing our stories on the sky,
like the grits in the coffee cup spinning around.

Coffee Readings 2

These grounds are dry.
Time must have stopped.

But inside the cup, what might be a mountain
is flying into the sky.
Simply a symbol? Of anxiety perhaps?
Because when mountains fly they leave the world behind.

What the coffee says is,
take it slow. But take is easy
when taking it slow.

This may mean rebirth. A place
between earth and sky.
But there's a cat in the coffee grits and perhaps a pigeon too.

Other spaces might be ocean depths,
but there too is a new moon thin as a switchblade.

Or, from this angle, the moon
is a mirror where east is west, north south,
and a man's heart beats on the right.

A star shines beside that moon,
burning brighter in the moonwax.
Do you think the cup is starting to tell the truth?

Coffee Readings 3

Masked, anonymous in a crowd of centaurs,
a dwarf-angel or angel-dwarf
regards everything.

Fish and reflections of fish. Birds and reflections
of birds bursting into flame.

But birds bring bad news. Fish bring bad news.
Dwarf-angels and angel-dwarves bring bad news.
So beware the centaurs. Beware all who lean like italics.
For it is better to go unmasked than join the soul-suq in the sky.

Now, from the horizon
a man approaches. Hilarious
as the wind he sees in all directions,
banishing the birds, the fish, the fire,
the dwarf-angels and the angel-dwarves.
And in your heart the day lengthens by the step of the cockerel.

THE SAND ORCHESTRA

We keep looking
but Ulysses has not returned.

Maybe he'll arrive
driving an electric car,

maybe she's the crackhead
at the corner,

sand-coloured highlights
in her hair.

But why is it up to me
to carry the carnival?

The glitter's too heavy.
All this tinsel.

Yet listen...

Those muffled drums...
That velvet pedal on the bass drum...
Yes, sand behind means sand ahead.

When I was in the peace movement
we thought the monstrous white carbide star
would settle on our roofs
and fire like the hair of Blake's Christ
fuse our horizons

together. But in the morning there was only sand,
sullen-strange but no stranger,
silicon icon stealing along the limestone sill.

So how do I spend my time?
Listening to sand,
the sand that eats words
just as the wind
dines on dunes,
sand spittering like a rainstick.

Attention sand! I say.
But after all these years
sand ignores the sand man.

This is urgent, I cry.
But might as well be talking to myself.

This sand sounds a thousand zithers,
Silurian crwth, Blackfoot flute,
each string of the Paraguayan harp

and when the tide goes out
every footstep has a hissy fit.

Now, sand's aria is in the laptop
and in the camera,
sand's atoms
split,
        splitting.

Meanwhile the men
have come to recycle roadside platinum.

Yes, it is time to admit
there is no Jesus in geology
so maybe the sandgod
is the broompod
or the yellowhammer
or the thumping hare
red as a strawberry,
the hare not hunted here
one thousand years,
and sand it is that hefts the hod
that holds the new republic.

Alone, I'm always alone in these places.
Hail on the left side of my face,
sun on the right.

I come to a plateau, old
gold as a Wolves shirt,
but seek a greener
arena. And look here, a polished
Bechstein, its black sail on the horizon.

If there is alarm sand will sound it –
the rattle of sand pouring handfuls of herself
into an empty tin of throat pastilles.

Such music she makes,
ragged as a razorshell
across the mermaid's neck.

In the gutters, round the gateposts,
sand utters its own exequies.

Okay, after exhaustion sand summons extinction.
But what a place
to put a piano.